Roberto Guillermo Gomes

CASSANDRA EFFECT: Arctic "methane bomb" analysis

Consultation without response to scientists about an abrupt feedback of clathrate release in 2025/30

IN PLANETARY ECOLOGICAL EMERGENCY, THE POLES ARE DEFROSTING AND THE OCEANS CAN ASCEND SEVERAL MTS FROM 2025/30

Dr. James Hansen warns: **"The last time the planet was warmer was in the interglacial period, about 120,000 years ago, and the sea level was between 6 and 9 meters higher than the current one. If we let that happen again, we will lose all the coastal cities."**

What nobody needs is when, or how long it will take to raise the water 6 or more meters and how to get to zero carbon emissions immediately to avoid it, especially if the global ecosystem is already entering the irreversibility and feedback phase Natural positive, in terms of global warming. The planet is already 1.1° C hotter and the pollution will get even hotter, so the precondition of the Hansen prediction is fulfilled. Here we will try to make a response construct.

The report, "Paths of the terrestrial system in the Anthropocene," published in American Proceedings of the National Academy of Sciences, states that "greenhouse" temperatures could stabilize from 4 ° C to 5 ° C higher than preindustrial levels. The main author, Will Steffen, from the National University of Australia, said that if they reach 2° C, positive feedbacks will be triggered that will boost the warming, which can cause an increase in sea level of up to 60 meters. To avoid this, the report recommends a redirection of the administration of the Earth's system and resources. **That is, the consumer society and capitalism as we know it, no longer go. Either we change or we flood.**

For a stable thermal equilibrium of the planet, CO_2 must be reduced to 350 ppm. Or this, or the certain possibility of facing irreversible catastrophic effects. In other words, the solution is twofold, it consists in stopping the emission of CO_2 and extracting the current excess CO_2 in the atmosphere until returning to the point of "safe" planetary thermo equilibrium. We can do this, we still have the technological organization and resources available, but an extraordinary global effort is required, equivalent to or greater than that made during World War II. The fact is that we have not yet taken the magnitude of the problem seriously and have not reacted, during the last 40 years of scientific analysis and political debates on Global Warming.

The World Meteorological Organization (WMO) announced that the global average temperature of the Earth's surface in 2018 exceeded by around 1.1 ° C the levels of the pre-industrial era (1850-1900) and by 0.2 degrees with respect to the 2011-2015 period. **The predictions now suggest about a 10% chance that at least one year between 2020 and 2023 temporarily exceeds 1.5 ° C.** With 1.2 ° C more than in the pre-industrial era, 2016, marked by the influence of a powerful El Niño, remains the hottest year. Meanwhile, the Arctic is reheating at a rate twice as fast as the world average. In July 2019, 21 degrees Celsius was reached in Alert - the northernmost inhabited town on the planet, less than 900 km from the North Pole, when the maximum average there is 6.1° C, that is, there were 15° C more.

These data indicate that there is no longer material time or resources to avoid global warming of the planet at 1.5° C. This may occur between 2020 and 2023. The atmospheric concentration of CO_2 measured at the Mauna Loa observatory, of NOAA, in Hawaii it increased during 2015 by 3.05 parts per million (ppm). The current increase is 200 times faster than prehistoric records. What's worse, the atmospheric CO_2 level is already (May 2019) at 415 ppm, with an average annual increase of 2.75 ppm. If this percentage is not raised further, by 2030 it will reach 445.25 ppm. But considering the carbon and methane leaks of permafrost and underwater clathrates, plus the overconsumption of fossil fuels, we will exceed 450 ppm before 2030 and cross the threshold of the dreaded 2 ° C global average temperature. From there, to the massive thaw of Greenland. With temperatures slightly higher than the current ones in the Arctic, about 125,000 years ago, the ocean surface was between 4 to 8 meters higher.

NOAA indicates that the atmosphere is heating up as if it had 21% more CO_2, this is due to additional gases such as methane and nitrous oxide whose presence is increasing considerably. According to a recent study, melting Alaskan permafrost releases 12 times more nitrous oxide than previously calculated. It is a gas 300 times more potent than CO_2 in greenhouse and also dissolves ozone in the upper atmosphere. The volume being released is unknown.

With the albedo effect, the floating ice of the North Pole reflects 70% of the solar radiation. As they unfreeze in summers, the Arctic Ocean absorbs more than 90% of this radiation that it receives directly and overheats. If these waters raise their temperature 5° C, that will be enough to release the huge deposits of methane gas hydrates and start a catastrophic climate chain reaction. Each cubic meter of methane gas hydrate in the Arctic ocean bed stores about 164 m³ of methane gas at 1 pressure atmosphere (pressure at sea level). For now, Greenland is losing around 250 billion tons of ice a year, on average. A large mass is transferring from the earth to the oceans.

Arctic permafrost is rapidly thawing. In doing so, cliffs are produced in the form of cliffs the size of multi-storey buildings collapsed in the ground, where methane escapes. In the background you can see bones of mammoths and other Pleistocene animals that remained frozen for thousands of years. According to some estimates between 30% and 70% of permafrost can be defrosted before 2100. Only 10% of the carbon released is 150,000 million tons. Bacteria and viruses are also released from diseases that have already disappeared. In addition, the United States Geological Survey estimates that there are a total of 1,656,000 tons of mercury trapped in polar ice and permafrost, which is beginning to transfer to the food chain due to defrosting.

The problem with permafrost is the temperature rise in the Arctic. Three years ago the soil temperature was minus three degrees Celsius, after minus two, after minus one, it is now two positive degrees. With the aggravating fact that permafrost now accuses an active defrosting process throughout the year. Before, many thought that a maximum of 10% of permafrost would be lost in a period of 80 years. **"Many of our hypotheses are falling apart"**, says Róisín Commane, an atmospheric chemist at Columbia University who tracks carbon emissions by plane.

But everything is accelerating when the active layer stops freezing in winter. The added heat allows the microbes that consume the organic matter of the soil to continue acting and they emit carbon dioxide and methane all year long, the winter heat is melting the permafrost more quickly and the whole process is accelerating at an unpredictable rate. On the entire planet, permafrost is home to 1600 gigatons of carbon, almost double what is present in the atmosphere.

This new reality of global warming added by accelerating defrosting of permafrost, according to new research, suggests that we should reduce emissions eight years earlier than projected by the IPCC models.

The cost of accelerating global warming due to the loss of permafrost and methane release plus temperature rise will reach 70 trillion dollars, according to an article in the journal Nature Communications by researchers of the Higher Council for Scientific Research (CSIC)

Currently, permafrost covers one fifth of the earth's surface, mainly from Greenland, Alaska, Canada and Russia. In total, the IPCC estimates that between 37% and 81% of the current permafrost will be lost due to global warming.

The arctic platform of eastern Siberia (ESAS) is the largest and shallowest platform in the world's ocean with an average depth of around 50 m. With an area of 2,000,000 square kilometers, housing the largest reservoir of permafrost and methane gas hydrates. Doctors Shakhova and Semiletov study the sector and warn about its high instability. They indicate that when the permafrost layer is lost, methane release will begin. The natural warming added to the anthropogenic, cause permafrost degradation processes to levels that had never been seen before.

They explain that in some places of ESAS the underwater permafrost is reaching the defrosting point, which can lead to increasing methane emissions, moving from a linear tendency to an exponential one, determining a turning point according to the level of heating reached. Scientists indicate that within the ESAS 200,000 square kilometers are currently critical, since methane emissions are already observed.

It has been discovered that the submarine permafrost of the Siberian Arctic is already losing 14 centimeters per year, a decrease higher than the earth's permafrost. The feedback has already started.

Arctic permafrost accumulates almost 2 billion tons of organic carbon, almost half of all organic carbon stored in the Earth's soils.

Its release represents a major acceleration impact on global warming. If the temperature rises 2° C, 40% of the permafrost will be thawed, which will release methane gas which in turn will increase the temperature more and release more methane causing a positive feedback.

Atmospheric methane concentrates 1,845 parts per billion (ppmm), equivalent to 256% of its preindustrial level. There is 220 times less methane than carbon dioxide in the atmosphere. While nitrous oxide (N2O) accuses an atmospheric concentration of 328 ppmm, equivalent to 121% of pre-industrial levels.

Scientists warn that much of the Amazon is on its way to becoming a savanna. Upon reaching a certain level of deforestation, you can reach a point of transformation without return, a phenomenon called tipping point. If 25% of the Amazon forest disappears, this will cause the dry season and the temperature to increase, moving from the tropical forest to a savanna vegetation. Deforestation has already reached 17%. The Amazon produces 20% of the planet's oxygen and absorbs 1 billion tons of carbon dioxide per year. If it disappears in 30 to 50 years, there will be less oxygen in the air and more CO_2, raising the global average temperature to 1° C for this cause. And we are not considering the rainforests of Africa, Asia and the forests of Canada, Alaska and Siberia, affected by the increasingly intense and frequent fires.

If forest fires continue to intensify in Siberia, Alaska, Canada, Africa and especially in the Amazon, this will cause a global average temperature increase, tending to 1.5° C and increase the proportion of free CO_2 in the atmosphere to 430 ppm. This will require an immediate coordinated global action to avoid a major catastrophe.

According to the calculations of UNHCR (the UN agency for Refugees), in the next 50 years between 250 and 1 billion people will be forced to leave their homes and move to another region of their country or even to another State if the Being human does not stop climate change.

"The disasters caused by the climate in 2017 cost the world economy 320,000 million dollars and around 10,000 lives were lost," said Christiana Figueres, Executive Secretary of the United Nations Framework Convention on Climate Change. Since 1995, due to climatic catastrophes, some 606,000 people have died and

4,100 million have been injured or injured. Due to the rise of the sea and loss of territories, it is estimated that by 2100 there will be 2 billion climate refugees.

Due to an increase in droughts, floods and heat waves, there are between 26 and 40 million climate refugees per year. According to the UN by 2050 the figure will reach 200 million displaced, other sources cite one billion.

The planet has entered during the last five years in an active positive feedback process involving 4 natural systems and 3 anthropogenic systems. These are:

1. Defrosting of the floating ice of the North Pole and reducing the albedo effect, thereby reheating the waters of the Arctic Ocean and melting more ice and permafrost. Which accelerates the melting of the Greenland glacier massifs and the oceanic ascent.

2. Defrosting of permafrost in acceleration, with release to the atmosphere of carbon and methane gas and initiation of the release of clathrates or hydrates of underwater methane gas in the Arctic platform.

3. Increasingly massive and intense natural forest fires in Siberia, Alaska, Canada, Africa and the Amazon, caused by droughts and heat waves. This reduces the areas of continental CO_2 sinks, which are released into the atmosphere, accelerating warming.

4. Anthropogenic forest fires, either by burning before planting, by logging, by abandonment of branches, or by neglect leaving fires poorly extinguished.

5. Anthropogenic pollution is around 40 gigatons of CO_2 emissions in the world per year.

6. To this is added that the oceans are losing the capacity to absorb 31% of the CO_2 generated by man. Between 1994 and 2007 they captured 34 gigatons (billions of metric tons). Surfactants, an oily film that extends over the surface of the water reduces the exchange of carbon dioxide by up to 50%. As surface temperatures increase, this organic layer increases and causes a greater decrease in gas exchange between the atmosphere and the oceans. As the effect increases, there will be an inertial increase in CO_2 in the atmosphere.

7. Overpopulation, with 8,600 million inhabitants by 2030, presses with the overconsumption of food and energy until planetary resources are depleted and global warming accelerated. There is a direct cause and effect relationship.

The combination of all these feedback will result in rapid and uncontrolled heating, whose negative impact can be equated with a thermonuclear war. To stop it, it is necessary to drastically reduce carbon dioxide emissions and, as far as possible, extract the excess already released into the atmosphere. In 100 years we have poured into the air what took 500 million years to accumulate in the underground in the form of oil.

The installed renewable energy capacity is still not enough to cover the global energy demand and thus the thermal coal plants are operating at full capacity.

China, the US, the EU and India, these four powers, accumulate 60% of the planet's CO2. Except in the EU, strong increases in emissions are expected in 2019.

Since 2012, oil consumption has been increasing at an annual rate of 1%. Although the manufacturing of electric cars improves, they only add up to 5 million in the world, against more than 1.2 billion cars that run on fossil fuels, consuming 100 million barrels / day of oil in 2019. The world consumed 94 million barrels / day in 2016. In 2013, 90 million and this was already triple the consumption of just half a century ago. Reserves for 45 years, will be exhausted by 2072. That is to say in 2019 we go for the COP25 climate summit, full of promises to reduce carbon emissions and the reality of the fact is that we increasingly increase fuel consumption fossils and our dependence on them.

The good news is that the renewable energy park doubles every four years.

WHAT SCIENTISTS SAY

Peter Wadhams, Professor of Ocean Physics at the University of Cambridge: **"Most glaciologists studying the Greenland melt estimate that (in this century) there will be a meter or more of a rise (from sea level), perhaps much more." "The speed at which**

the Greenland ice sheet melts has greatly increased in recent years, due to the warmer air that arrives in summer from the Arctic Ocean." "The drainage glaciers began to suffer an acceleration facilitated by the melting water to the point that, at present, some are advancing at double speed and deposit much more ice in the sea, in the form of icebergs."

Carol Ramussen of the NASA Earth Science News Team: **"Many of Greenland's great glaciers are at greater risk of melting due to what was previously thought, according to the new maps of the seabed around Greenland created by an international research team. "**

Jane Beitler, Director of the Science Communication Group, National Snow and Ice Data Center (NSIDC), University of Colorado, Boulder: **"The Greenland ice sheet contains enough ice to raise the sea level twenty-four feet (7.3 m), if the whole were melted".**

Eric Rignot, Professor of Terrestrial System Science at the University of California, Irvine, and principal investigator of Radar Science and Engineering Section of NASA's Jet Propulsion Laboratory, Pasadena, California: **"The Underwater Valleys (of Greenland) make glaciers more susceptible to rapid and prolonged setbacks. It is a radical change in relation to sea level. The sea level rise due to Greenland will be higher than the current models project".**

Mathieu Morlighem, associate professor of Earth System Science, University of California, Irvine, co-founder of the Ice Layer System Model: **"We now know that Greenland melting will not cease in a decade or so. It will continue to thaw. As the ice recedes, it will maintain contact with the ocean because it will follow it inland. "**

Kevin Schaefer, Tingjun Zhang, Lori Bruhwiler, L. Andrew P. Barrett, National Snow and Ice Data Center of the University of Colorado at Boulder, National Oceanic and Atmospheric Administration (NOAA), USA: **"The merger and The emission of the currently frozen carbon in the permafrost will increase the atmospheric concentration of CO2 and amplify the surface heating to initiate a positive feedback (permafrost carbon feedback, PCF) ... We predict that the PCF will change the**

Arctic from the sink state of carbon to the carbon source from the middle of the 2020s, and is intense enough to override 42-88% of the effect of all terrestrial carbon sinks. The fusion and decomposition of permafrost is irreversible ... Our estimate can be conservative, since it does not take into account the amplified heating of the surface due to the PCF itself."

The decrease in the albedo effect in the North Pole causes the reflection of solar radiation to decrease from 0.6 to 0.1, increasing the solar energy absorbed by the Arctic Ocean, which impacts to accelerate the defrosting of Greenland and precipitate the release of the immense deposits of underwater methane gas hydrates when the water warms. Here the first positive feedback effect is presented with reduction of the albedo effect, overheating of ocean waters and acceleration of thaw.

On July 23, 2012 there was a strong solar storm and great activity in our star, this coincided with 97% of the Greenland ice sheet covered by meltwater due to a heat wave parked on the island. Currently, the ice in that territory melts six times faster than in the 1980s. The Greenland ice sheet lost almost 4 billion tons of ice since 2002. In 2012 the loss was 450,000 million tons, raising the level of sea up to 2 millimeters. Every year 300 cubic kilometers of ice are lost from the Greenland layer. During the month of July 2019 alone, the Greenland ice sheet lost 197,000 million tons of ice. The record for the lowest sea ice surface in the Arctic, which was around 3.3 million square kilometers, also happened in 2012.

The melting of Greenland is accelerating with direct discharge to the ocean and rapid melting of coastal glaciers. The surface water makes its way through holes called "mills", which connect with the bed of rock, advances on it to the base of the glacial tongues and reduces friction with the rock bed, accelerating the descent of the glaciers that are they fragment forming icebergs in the ocean. According to the latest measurements, the rate of descent has doubled in the last decade, accelerating the regression of drainage glaciers.

On the other hand, Greenland's glaciers are blackening, covering soot and seaweed, making the glacier less reflective, so it absorbs the sun's rays more. This speeds up the heating and in turn leads to an even greater melt.

Since 1880 global warming has increased sea level by 20 centimeters, increasing the chances of damaging properties on the coast by storm surge. According to Climate Central, the risk of flooding can double by 2030. In the United States alone, almost 5 million people live in 2.6 million homes less than 1.20 meters above high tide, a level below the water line. Flood by the end of the century, which is expected to be up to a 2-meter rise in the oceans. During the last 25 years the sea has risen 7 centimeters, so if the ascent were constant the rise would have to wait for 2100 another 23 centimeters, totaling 43 centimeters. But the phenomenon of the thaw of the poles is accelerating from linear to exponential, because there are positive feedbacks involved in the process. Meanwhile, the average rate of increase from 1993 to date is 3.2 mm per year, from May 2014 to 2019 it has increased to 5 mm per year. In ten years, an average annual level of about 4 mm has been recorded. About twice the average speed of the previous 80 years. The sea level has increased 82.8 mm since 1993. If the global average temperature reaches 2º C, positive feedback will be activated and an oceanic rise of one millimeters per year will change to centimeters. **The speed at which the ice will respond to this new condition is ignored.**

During the Optimum Climate Pliocene, with global average temperatures up to 4º C higher than the pre-industrial levels, four million years ago, the sea level was 23.5 meters higher, the ice sheets of Greenland and Antarctica having collapsed Western. If the temperature now rises this story can be repeated. Today Greenland loses about 270 billion tons of ice per year, 70% by thawing, 30% by masses of ice that break apart and another 30% by winter rains located in the south, but which are gradually extending northward in the as the temperature rises so the percentage incidence will increase.

The thermohaline current (or conveyor belt) that influences the regulation of the global climate, especially Europe, is showing signs of slowing down and pre-collapse, due to the rapid thaw in Greenland and the pouring of fresh water into the ocean along with a higher water temperature of the Sea in northern Europe. Professor Peter Wadhams based on these changes predicts an increase of 4º C in continental Europe at the end of the century. The Intergovernmental Panel on Climate Change (IPCC) that advises the UN has gone on to include the rapid defrosting of Greenland in its projections and now predicts an oceanic rise of 1 meter or more by the end of the century, which puts it at risk to populations residing in the low coastal areas. A large part of the world's population (600 million) resides in coastal cities. Cities consume about two thirds of the world's energy, and are responsible for more than 70% of global greenhouse gas emissions.

Whadhams also warns of the imminent risk of abrupt fusion of marine permafrost, which contains methane gas, which acts as a cork for the huge deposits of clathrates or methane gas hydrates (CH_4), a greenhouse gas 23 times more potent than CO_2 The melting of the floating ice of the North Pole, the absence of the albedo effect and as a consequence the overheating of the Arctic Ocean, would cause the rapid release of these underwater reservoirs. Chimneys of methane are already being observed, with fusion of hydrates in the East Siberian Sea, as well as in the seas of Laptev and Kara. This is happening now, now. Whadhams calculates that these gases once released can produce an extra heating of 0.6° C. But everything will depend on the amount of carbon and methane released in the process.

The Northern Hemisphere where the most productive farmland on the planet is located, is being affected by droughts, floods, cold or heat waves. This is due to the jet stream that separates the Arctic from air masses at lower latitudes, and which has now slowed down, is slower and allows local weather systems to be prolonged from a single phenomenon. If this effect persists, world food production can be in serious danger, causing famine situations, rising food prices and wars. **We are already at the gates of the worst possible scenarios and continue without acting.**

The floating ice of the North Pole accused 8 million square kilometers in the period of greatest decline (September). Today it has come to contain 3-4 million square kilometers and half the thickness of ice. Thus the summer ice has been reduced to a quarter of the volume it had in the seventies of the last century. There is practically no more multiannual ice, formed several years before with large ridges. Now almost all the ice is formed during the current season and reaches an average thickness of 1.5 meters with small ridges. It is estimated that the ice that forms during a single winter can melt completely in a single summer. And then the albedo effect will disappear and the ocean waters of the sector will overheat and may cause the release of immense deposits of underwater methane gas hydrates. This will accelerate the heating between 25 and 500% depending on the magnitude of the gas release. Positive feedbacks will be triggered some foreseeable and others totally unknown now. We do not have the data to be able to create predictive models of the phenomenon. We are entering a horizon of total climate insecurity. We do know that with less sea ice, snow on the Arctic coastal lands thaws faster in spring, due to the emergence of warmer air fronts that reach the coast from the clear sea. That was how in June 2012 there were 6 million kilometers less than in 1980. The decrease in the albedo of floating ice and snow, contribute 30% to global warming, accelerating the process.

Due to the warmer air that arrives in summer from the Arctic Ocean, the Greenland ice sheet is accelerating its defrosting rate, with which the sea level rise is increasing. The IPCC in 2007 made the prediction that the waters would rise 30 centimeters by 2100, then updated it to 60-90 centimeters. Other studies define climbs of several meters. The point is that as long as there is floating ice on the North Pole, the water temperature cannot go up from 0° C. But when all the ice disappears in summer, the sea surface can be heated up to 7° C, and on the marine platform that heat it will reach the seabed melting the underwater permafrost and methane gas hydrates. A third of the Arctic Ocean is made up of marine platforms between 50 and 100 meters, so the amount of methane stored is immense. If the 2,850.00 km3 of Greenland's ice melted, there would be a sea level rise of 7.2 m. **Many scientists agree that if the global average temperature rises 2° C, Greenland will defrost completely.**

Clatrato (from the Latin clathratus, "surrounded or protected, lattice") is a type of molecule that traps and retains another type of molecule. A gaseous hydrate, for example a clathrate, is formed by a water molecule that contains a gas. It is a non-stoichiometric compound of 2-9 Angstrom. Thus frozen water creates cells that contain gas molecules linked by hydrogen bonds. Clathrates are formed with various gases. With CH4 the clathrates are stabilized at a certain pressure and temperature on the seabed. These cells are unstable if they are empty and collapse forming conventional ice. There are two dodecahedrons with twelve molecules of water, it is one molecule of methane (CH4) for every 5.75 molecules of water. If a large amount of methane enters the atmosphere it will act efficiently as a greenhouse gas for 10 to 20 years, until it dissipates by oxidation in water and carbon dioxide. A 10% escape of methane contained in underwater clathrates would have the impact of multiplying by 10 the current concentration of CO2 in the atmosphere.

Clathrates accumulate on the continental margins of the world's oceans, that is, on the slopes, which plunge deep into the continents. It would be about 12 billion tons of methane gas.

Scientific estimates indicate that the energy stored in the clathrates is at least twice the total energy stored in the fossil fuel reserves present in the earth's crust. The figure is around 21 x 10^{15} Nm3. This resource is considered as a future energy reserve to be exploited.

There are 164 cubic meters of methane gas for every cubic meter of methane hydrate, with only 0.84 cubic meters of water. It is flammable ice. Exposed to fire begins to burn.

The largest marine methane pond on Earth spans from the coast of Central America to Hawaii in the Tropical Pacific Ocean. These hydrates can also be destabilized as ocean water increases temperature.

The Upper Paleocene Thermal Maximum, 55.8 million years ago, one of the most significant periods of climate change of the Cenozoic era, which altered the oceanic and atmospheric circulation, caused a mass extinction of species. One of the hypotheses about its origin is the release of methane that was stored in the clathrates of ocean sediments, which released large amounts of carbon into the atmosphere. The mass extinction of the Permian-Triassic, which occurred approximately 250 million years ago, also involves the release of large quantities of greenhouse gases trapped in the ocean floor in the form of methane hydrates. The current human contamination by CO_2 pushes towards what is called clathrates rifle or abrupt release of underwater methane, with enough potential to raise the global average temperature to an additional ~ 5 / 6° C.

The temperature on the planet is rising, this causes a positive feedback effect that defrosts permafrost, releasing CO_2 and methane, further increasing the temperature. In the thermokarst lakes (lakes formed in the depressions left by the defrosting of the permafrost) the warmer surface water accelerates the defrosting of the bottom permafrost, accelerating the process. The permafrost area is approximately 15 million km2 in the northern hemisphere. There are 850 gigatons of carbon in the atmosphere, the equivalent in weight to 100,000 school buses. The carbon frozen in permafrost doubles that present in the atmosphere today.

For the UN Intergovernmental Panel on Climate Change (IPCC) it is crucial to limit the global average temperature increase to a maximum of 1.5 degrees Celsius. It is based on more than 6,000 scientific references. If we continue to pollute as we are up to now, we are on the way to an increase between 3º C to 5º C. The limit of 1.5º C could be exceeded in less than 12 years, according to the IPCC. To achieve this goal, it recommends investing 2.5% of the world's GDP annually and reducing CO_2 emissions by 45% by 2030 and reaching zero emissions by 2050. The plan includes that renewable energies provide up to 85 % of the world's electricity by 2050 and that an area the size of Australia be dedicated to energy crops. Among the changes to be adopted at an individual level to mitigate warming, it suggests: 1. Buy less meat, milk, cheese and butter and more locally produced seasonal foods (in addition to wasting less food). 2. Drive electric cars and walk or use the bike for short trips. 3. Take trains and buses instead of airplanes. 4. Resort to videoconferences instead of traveling for work reasons. 5. Dry clothes in the sun instead of using dryers. 6. Better insulate houses to reduce dependence on heating and / or air conditioners. 7. Demand a low carbon footprint in all consumer products.

WAKE UP TO REALITY

The idea that we still have time to avoid the climatic tragedy is wrong, we are running out of time. We must act immediately. This paper tries to raise awareness about this.
It is not about panicking, but about reacting assertively, enlightened by science and with the heart defending the life of all beings on the planet.

What is happening is a consequence of the accumulated failures on the political decision-making system. The forms of organization of the current governments have failed and have led us to an intense predation of Mother Nature, to the point that we have unbalanced the natural forces in an almost irreversible way. If we want a second chance, we must immediately change our system of economic, political and technological organization, making it neutral with the environment.

The goal of reducing carbon emissions by 45% by 2030 is feasible, but reaching zero emissions by 2050 presents technological problems. Wind and solar energy are intermittent, when there is no wind or it is cloudy they do not collect energy, so they rely on large batteries to store reserve energy. Currently all available batteries on the planet are enough to charge an hour of the gross world generation of electric power. So at present we do not have the technology to achieve the goal of zero emissions unless we complement nuclear energy, be it fission or fusion.

In September 2019, more than 1,000 cities in 19 countries have declared weather emergencies, representing more than 224 million people, according to data from The Climate Mobilization. Organizations representing more than 7,000 universities on six continents have declared a climate emergency and have agreed on a plan to address the crisis and become carbon neutral in 2030. This should mean taking immediate measures against fossil fuel consumption, but everything continues same. There are almost ~ 5/10 million climate change activists in the world compared to 7,727 million indifferent people. We are not winning. We need you to participate to make a difference, we are in the middle of a 7th mass extinction, we can still stop it.

The world clings to the prediction of an oceanic rise of 1.2 meters by 2100. We warn that reality can change if permafrost is released and this triggers underwater methane gas hydrates. They are billions of stored tons that will be released into the atmosphere and will increase the temperature abruptly to no less than 6° C and up to 12° C at both poles. These temperature jumps are already happening locally and not yet globally. This will cause the accelerated thaw of both caps, the waters can rise almost 60 meters. You can pass? Permafrost is already defrosting in quantity. There will be feedback. We are facing a highly unstable climate system that we understand as the phenomenon progresses, this is the measure of scientific limitation. In other words, the predictions fail, because the models are loaded with incomplete data. **Defrosting is accelerating and it took almost everyone by surprise. And it will accelerate even more.**

WHAT'S GOING ON?

Greenland was defrosted in the middle of June 2019, and the visual test is the photo taken by Danish scientist Steffen Olsen. In the picture, a group of dogs drag two sleds over a layer of melted ice. According to the Danish Meteorological Institute, the thermometers had reached 17.3º C: an unusually high temperature for northern Greenland. In the same month the ocean waters had risen 5 degrees, while in August the historical temperature difference reached 10 degrees, repeating the 2012 record. Then although the global average temperature has not yet risen to 6º C, at the local level there are already pronounced jumps in the thermometers, in sensitive areas covered by previously permanent ice, which now begin to thaw rapidly. Here it is possible to warn about the data of the increase of 5 degrees in the temperature of the oceanic waters, it is the threshold that is required for the release of underwater methane gas hydrates.

EVERYTHING CAN HAPPEN

Antonio Guterres, the UN Secretary General, said **"Arctic permafrost is melting decades earlier than in the worst scenarios,"** threatening to unblock large amounts of the powerful methane from greenhouse gases.
This can accelerate the release of the immense underwater deposits of methane gas hydrate in the Arctic Ocean bed and increase the global average temperature between 4º to 6º C and up to 12º C in

both poles… **No one knows exactly when or how the worst can happen.**

WHAT TO DO?

For the UN advisory scientists, the three most important measures to avoid this planetary catastrophe are:

1. An investment of 2.5% of world GDP for 2 decades, to mitigate climate change.

2. Reduce carbon dioxide (CO2) emissions by 45% by 2030. (We recommend 80% now, due to the danger of the "Arctic methane pump").

3. That an extension of land the size of Australia be dedicated to the production of clean energy. (It is more rational to reduce global consumption by turning off the lights of all cities after 8 pm).

A UN report warns that, even applying the measures of the Paris Agreement, the region surrounding the North Pole will undergo radical changes in the coming decades. Arctic winter temperatures will rise from 3 ° C to 5 ° C by 2050 and from 5 ° C to 9 ° C by 2080. It is estimated that Arctic sea ice has decreased 40%, and climate models predict that, at the current rate of CO_2 emissions, ice will disappear during the Arctic summers by the 2030s. Arctic permafrost is expected to reduce 45% compared to its current state. Globally, these frozen soils contain 1,672 Tt (teratons, or billions of tons) of carbon, an amount similar to all the carbon currently present in the atmosphere and there are 4×10^{16} cubic meters of methane gas in the sediments of the seabed. While Antarctica lost 169,000 million tons of ice annually between 1992 and 2017.

The increase in melting is expected to contribute significantly to carbon dioxide and methane emissions, and the resulting warming in turn will lead to even greater thaw, an effect known as "positive feedback." To this is added the fact that due to the constant rate of human contamination, 450 ppm of atmospheric CO_2 will be reached in 2030 and the global average temperature will rise 2º C. This will accelerate the defrosting of the permafrost and the release of the methane content, further increasing the planet temperature

The clathrate rifle hypothesis is a scientific theory that argues that rising sea temperatures can lead to a sudden release of methane from methane clathrate deposits located at the ocean floor. This would cause an alteration of the environment of the oceans and the atmosphere of the Earth, similar to what could have happened according to the theory of Permian-Triassic extinction, and in the maximum thermal of the Paleocene-Eocene. Against the situation chart, reducing carbon emissions by 45% by 2030 may be insufficient. It is advisable to do it at 80% immediately. Not staggered, but now, immediately, making a maximum effort. If this is not done, positive feedback already unleashed from climate change cannot be stopped. Time is up, or we do it or tragedy, it is our choice. Read Drs' reports: James Hansen, Lowell Stott and Will Steffen. If the IPCC predicts dramatic climate change, they project a catastrophic one at full speed.

WHAT IS IT ABOUT?

Global solutions for climate change are composed of local microsolutions. For this, heterogeneous coalitions are necessary. **2% for the Planet** is a global network of national and international multisectoral coalitions committed to supporting the climate objectives of each country. We intend to connect cities, states, the private sector, investors, students, universities, scientists, politicians and civil society nationally and globally so that they can join efforts and wills to coordinate actions with their national governments, to carry out effective actions of positive climate change.

URGENT AND FAST ACTIONS NEEDED

Limiting the increase in the global average temperature to 1.5 ° C is within reach, but only if we take firm action now at all levels of government and in all segments of society. The North Pole is already defrosting and when it is completely defrosted in the summers, huge deposits of methane gas hydrates will begin to be released underwater, which will cause the global average temperature to rise by 6° C and up to 12° C at both poles , which will cause a global meltdown and irreversible flooding in all coastal cities. Business leaders, academic institutions, regional and local governments and civil society play a vital role in complying with the Paris COP21 Agreement and in ensuring a secure future for all.

WHY 2% OF GLOBAL GDP?

Our actions in the coming decades may involve the risk of a disruption of economic and social activity during the rest of this century and next, on a scale similar to that of the Great Wars and the Great Depression due to Global Warming. This is the conclusion of the report by economist Sir Nicholas Stern commissioned by the United Kingdom government and published on October 30, 2006.

Its main conclusions are that an investment equivalent to 1% of world GDP is needed to mitigate the effects of climate change and that if this investment is not made, the world will be exposed to a recession that could reach 20% of world GDP. The report also suggests the imposition of ecotic to minimize socioeconomic imbalances.

The United Nations Environment Program (UNEP) proposed to allocate 2% of annual global GDP by applying: 0.5% to the natural capital sectors (forests, agriculture, freshwater and fisheries); 1% to improve energy efficiency and the use of renewable energies (mainly applied to construction, industry and transport), and the remaining percentage to waste and public transport.

With 2% of the world's GDP, 500 billion dollars per year can be used to end hunger, pandemics and alleviate extreme poverty worldwide. Also activate a planting program of 30 billion trees per year to capture CO_2 in the trunks and then bury them, returning to 350 ppm of this free greenhouse gas in the atmosphere and returning to normal global climate. It will also be possible to invest heavily in fusion reactors to replace the energy matrix by replacing thermoelectric plants that burn gas, oil and coal. And accelerate the manufacture of hydrogen and electric cars.

To coordinate global tasks, a planetary ecological government will be required under the Global Direct Digital Democracy system, advised by a Science Council composed of scientists from five continents. Global positive change will further expand the rights of planetary citizenship and impose English as a second international language.

*** For more data read "E-Gobierno Mundial -2% para el Planeta"**

WHERE WILL THE FUNDS COME FROM?

To integrate 2% of world GDP, new taxes can be imposed or reallocated. A 0.3% rate will be applied on the international and national financial system. If such a rate is insufficient, an 8% tax will be applied on the profits of the oil companies operating in each country, and if this is not enough, it will be appealed to collect up to 5% of the net profit of the multinationals. **US $ 1 trillion is available to be seized in subsidies to the oil, coal and gas sector annually.** And the armies of the planet spend 2 billion dollars a year. **Having a planetary army would save 1 trillion.**

The secondary objective is to combat drug trafficking, terrorism, human trafficking and organized corruption. The whole society will tend to stabilize at a new level of higher order in a new concept of greater balance with Nature on a decontaminated planet with a human population tending towards stability. The objective to reduce overpopulation is: one child per family and achieve a reduction to 5 billion inhabitants, which is the limit that the planet can support.

2% of global GDP is equivalent to almost 2 trillion dollars per year.

The current global consumption system is inconsistent: 2% of world GDP goes into military spending, another 5% in corruption, another 2% in money laundering, another 2% in smoking, another 2% in drug trafficking and another 2% in mobile telephony (15% of total GDP in superfluous expenses)… While the system refuses to contribute a 2% fund to save the entire planet… The United Nations Environment Program (UNEP) advises allocate 2% for the green economy ... **what are we waiting for ?!**

A LITTLE LISTEN TO US ...

The "E-World Government-2% of GDP for the Planet" project, by architect Roberto Gomes, dates from 2009.
The United Nations has adopted the following initiatives:

1.-World ecological emergency declaration.
2.-Claim a fund of 2% of annual global GDP for the green economy (through UNEP).
3.-Claim the embargo on global fossil fuel subsidies.

4.-Prohibit the construction of new thermal plants.
5.-Set the heating limit to 1.5º C.
6.-Replace the vehicles with electric ones.
7.-Invest heavily in alternative energy replacement.

What's missing:

Define a centralized ecological world government to coordinate global actions. Giving power to planetary citizenship through direct digital democracy. Ensure peace across the globe by creating a planetary coalition Army (green helmets). Eradicate hunger forever, abolish extreme poverty. Redistribute the greatest wealth that robots and AI will contribute through a minimum annuity to the entire population. Establish a second universal language (English). One child per family. Intensify the investment for the tuning of fusion reactors. Elimination of money, supplanting it by units of qualified time. Decontaminate, save ecosystems and plant 500 billion trees to capture CO_2 and subsequently bury the logs cyclically.

IMAGINE A BETTER WORLD

With the Master Plan to Save the Planet we project a world without hunger, without poverty, without pandemics, without borders, with 2 languages, one universal, with only one Army and therefore without wars, without currency and without capital, with an E- Planetary Government under the Global Direct Digital Democracy system, where the citizens of the world vote all the laws and designate and dismiss the authorities of the other central powers, advised by a Science Council composed of the best scientists from all continents, with the work in charge of cybernetics and AI, redistributing the benefits through a life annuity to the entire population employed through creative leisure and social, artistic and scientific service. Adults, children and the elderly, meditating and expanding their minds to Cosmic Quantum Intelligence. With the planet greening through the recovery of forests and oceans, along with the protection of biodiversity. Finally, man living in peace and brotherhood with each other and in harmony between science,

truction of new thermal plants.
mit to 1.5° C.
cles with electric ones.
alternative energy replacement.

zed ecological world government to coordinate
ving power to planetary citizenship through direct
. Ensure peace across the globe by creating a
Army (green helmets). Eradicate hunger forever,
overty. Redistribute the greatest wealth that robots
ribute through a minimum annuity to the entire
lish a second universal language (English). One
Intensify the investment for the tuning of fusion
tion of money, supplanting it by units of qualified
ate, save ecosystems and plant 500 billion trees to
subsequently bury the logs cyclically.

BETTER WORLD

Plan to Save the Planet we project a world without
poverty, without pandemics, without borders, with 2
universal, with only one Army and therefore without
currency and without capital, with an E- Planetary
nder the Global Direct Digital Democracy system,
ens of the world vote all the laws and designate and
thorities of the other central powers, advised by a
il composed of the best scientists from all continents
in charge of cybernetics and AI, redistributing the
gh a life annuity to the entire population employe
ve leisure and social, artistic and scientific service
n and the elderly, meditating and expanding the
mic Quantum Intelligence. With the planet greenir
recovery of forests and oceans, along with th
biodiversity. Finally, man living in peace a
with each other and in harmony between scien

URGENT AND FAST ACTIONS NEEDED

Limiting the increase in the global average temperature to 1.5 ° C is within reach, but only if we take firm action now at all levels of government and in all segments of society. The North Pole is already defrosting and when it is completely defrosted in the summers, huge deposits of methane gas hydrates will begin to be released underwater, which will cause the global average temperature to rise by 6° C and up to 12° C at both poles , which will cause a global meltdown and irreversible flooding in all coastal cities. Business leaders, academic institutions, regional and local governments and civil society play a vital role in complying with the Paris COP21 Agreement and in ensuring a secure future for all.

WHY 2% OF GLOBAL GDP?

Our actions in the coming decades may involve the risk of a disruption of economic and social activity during the rest of this century and next, on a scale similar to that of the Great Wars and the Great Depression due to Global Warming. This is the conclusion of the report by economist Sir Nicholas Stern commissioned by the United Kingdom government and published on October 30, 2006.

Its main conclusions are that an investment equivalent to 1% of world GDP is needed to mitigate the effects of climate change and that if this investment is not made, the world will be exposed to a recession that could reach 20% of world GDP. The report also suggests the imposition of ecotic to minimize socioeconomic imbalances.

The United Nations Environment Program (UNEP) proposed to allocate 2% of annual global GDP by applying: 0.5% to the natural capital sectors (forests, agriculture, freshwater and fisheries); 1% to improve energy efficiency and the use of renewable energies (mainly applied to construction, industry and transport), and the remaining percentage to waste and public transport.

With 2% of the world's GDP, 500 billion dollars per year can be used to end hunger, pandemics and alleviate extreme poverty worldwide. Also activate a planting program of 30 billion trees per year to capture CO_2 in the trunks and then bury them, returning to 350 ppm of this free greenhouse gas in the atmosphere and returning to normal global climate. It will also be possible to invest heavily in fusion reactors to replace the energy matrix by replacing thermoelectric plants that burn gas, oil and coal. And accelerate the manufacture of hydrogen and electric cars.

To coordinate global tasks, a planetary ecological government will be required under the Global Direct Digital Democracy system, advised by a Science Council composed of scientists from five continents. Global positive change will further expand the rights of planetary citizenship and impose English as a second international language.

* For more data read "E-Gobierno Mundial -2% para el Planeta"

WHERE WILL THE FUNDS COME FROM?

To integrate 2% of world GDP, new taxes can be imposed or reallocated. A 0.3% rate will be applied on the international and

national financial syste
be applied on the pro
country, and if this is n
5% of the net profit of th
**to be seized in subs
annually.** And the armie
Having a planetary arm

The secondary objective
human trafficking and or
tend to stabilize at a new
greater balance with Nat
human population tending
overpopulation is: one chil
billion inhabitants, which is

**2% of global GDP is equi
year.**

The current global consump
GDP goes into military spen
2% in money laundering, ar
drug trafficking and another
GDP in superfluous expens
contribute a 2% fund to save t
Environment Program (UNEP
economy ... **what are we waiti**

A LITTLE LISTEN TO U

The "E-World Government-2%
architect Roberto Gomes, dates
The United Nations has adopted

1.-World ecological emergency de
2.-Claim a fund of 2% of annual g (through UNEP).
3.-Claim the embargo on global fos

4.-Prohibit the cons
5.-Set the heating l
6.-Replace the veh
7.-Invest heavily in

What's missing:

Define a centrali
global actions. Gi
digital democracy
planetary coalition
abolish extreme p
and AI will cont
population. Estab
child per family.
reactors. Elimina
time. Decontamir
capture CO_2 and

IMAGINE A

With the Maste
hunger, without
languages, one
wars, without
Government u
where the citiz
dismiss the au
Science Counc
with the work
benefits throu
through creat
Adults, childr
minds to Cos
through the
protection o
brotherhood

technology and Nature ... Just wake up, unite and together make it a reality.

CASANDRA EFFECT: AUTISTS OR SUICIDES?, NO ONE ANSWERS

On October 8, 2018, the Intergovernmental Panel on Climate Change (IPCC) published Global Warming of 1.5 ° C, making a comparison between the consequences of the temperature rise of 1.5 ° C and of 2° C.

The report also indicates that a global acceleration of the climatic action, much more intense and combined, is required to keep the warming in line with 1.5 ° C (partly because the planet presents a trajectory of temperature increase on the way up until 3 ° C on average for 2100).

What is the problem with this report? It does not contemplate the defrosting of the Arctic permafrost and the release of the immense deposits of underwater methane gas hydrates in the Arctic Ocean, which will bubble to the surface when the global average temperature rises. This will begin to occur when the barrier of 450 ppm of CO_2 is crossed, currently at 415 (May 2019) and rising 2.75 ppm annually and with a percentage increase due to an increase in overpopulation (we will be 8,600 million in 2030) and pressure of overconsumption of fossil fuels. This puts us on a timeline about the year 2030 or a little earlier. Then, according to the words of Dr. James Hansen, the global average temperature will rise another degree, adding 2° C and as a consequence the oceans will rise the first 6 meters, with both poles defrosting in an accelerated way and flooding all the coastal cities, with the consequence of 600 to one billion people evacuated.

Permafrost can release around 150,000 million tons of CO_2 annually and trigger an increase in global temperature that causes the release of underwater clathrates. The defrosting of the Arctic permafrost, the part of frozen soil that stores methane and CO_2 and therefore will emit even more greenhouse gases into the atmosphere when it falls apart, will accelerate climate change. This thaw can cost up to 70 billion euros to the world economy.

About a quarter of the northern hemisphere is covered by permafrost. Now, these beds of earth, rock and sediments that were permanently frozen are no longer so: they are melting at an alarming rate.

At the first signs of thawing, scientists rushed to monitor the emissions of the two most influential anthropogenic greenhouse gases: carbon dioxide and methane, but to date the threat of the third most important gas - nitrous oxide - went unnoticed.

Now, a report reveals that nitrous oxide emissions caused by the melting of Alaskan permafrost are about 12 times higher than previously thought. Since nitrous oxide is about 300 times more potent than carbon dioxide, this revelation could mean that the Arctic - and our global climate - would be in more danger than we thought.

CARBON UNDERWATER RESERVES

A report published in the Environmental Research Letters magazine states that 17,000 years ago, at the end of the Pleistocene era, carbon gases, which are produced naturally, were released from the seabed by an increase in the global average temperature and this caused the end of the Ice Age.

The geological processes involved with climatic variations can dramatically alter the seabed carbon cycle and cause a total change on ecosystems.

Due to the pollution exerted by the human being, the oceans are overheating and already the immense submarine carbon reservoirs are releasing greenhouse gases into the atmosphere, within a process that is accelerated within a positive feedback. If this intensifies the amount of carbon that can reach the atmosphere would be twice what it currently contains, so the temperature can stabilize at 7º C more.

"We are using the past as a way to anticipate the future," said Lowell Stott, a professor of Earth sciences at the University of Southern California (USA) and lead author of the study, cited by the phys.org portal.

Methane levels began to increase with the industrial revolution and are now 2.5 times higher than they have ever been naturally. These levels have caused a third of the increase observed in global average temperatures in relation to the pre-industrial era. If we want to reduce methane emissions, we have to understand where they come from. Calculating all the different sources is tremendously complicated, but it becomes even more difficult when natural and human-produced emissions occur at the same time and through similar processes.

To make matters worse, climate change caused by humans could destabilize permafrost or ice-like sediments called gas hydrates (or clathrates), which could release more methane than any human activity and enhance climate change. This scenario has been the main hypothesis behind other global warming in history (the " clathrates rifle") and future climate change out of control (the so-called "Arctic methane bomb"). How likely are these events to occur?

Some studies deny the possibility that the "methane pump" can be activated, others affirm it. But using common sense, the concrete thing is that permafrost is already defrosting at full speed and releasing methane gas, helping to reheat the planet more quickly and shortening the times for an organized preventive reaction of humanity.

What to do?

About the danger of the "methane bomb" that may explode before 2030 ending this civilization, by e-mail we communicate with the United Nations Secretary General, Antonio Guterres, asking him to ask the IPCC scientists to investigate on the subject and make a detailed report that serves as a standard to define action policies. Guterres did not answer.

Nor did authorities from UNEP, Greenpeace, WWF, Bill Gates, Greta Thumberg and the IPCC itself respond, as well as many others contacted. It is the Kassandra Effect that does not give credit to the reality of the facts. They hold on to the hope of a less threatening and less compromising future, which prevents them from applying totally unpopular measures.

Those who did respond were the organizers of COP25, in Chile, who said they took note of the matter.

Why is the subject so traumatic?

The official speech of the United Nations, of which Guterres is a spokesperson, is to reduce carbon emissions to 45% by 2030 and zero emissions by 2050. But if clathrates are released by 2030 or earlier, the global average temperature can to rise up to 6º C and 12º C in both poles, with which there will be an accelerated defrosting of both caps and the oceans can ascend up to 60 meters.

Faced with this new panorama of maximum emergency, the urgent measures to be applied in the world are:

1. Prohibit vehicles that release greenhouse gases.
2. Replace in the short and medium term the plants that work by burning oil and coal.
3. Prohibit tourism.
4. Dramatically reduce airline flights.
5. Turn off all city lights after 8 pm.
6. Reduce the consumption of red meat.
7. Move from intensive to organic crops.
8. Accelerate fusion reactors.
9. Invest heavily in alternative energies.
10. Stop consuming in short cycles, to produce with quality and with high durability products.
11. Replace individual vehicles in cities with collective urban transport.
12. Reforest by planting 30 billion trees per year.
We have run out of time. We must apply emergency measures, equivalent to the economic organization of the United States during

World War II, both in the rationing of energy and in the goods of production and consumption. At the same time sequester carbon and cool the Earth to safe levels, returning to 350 ppm of CO_2. We must opt for high-speed electrified railroads, fossil fuel replacement and cities without cars. Also move from industrial agriculture to localized regeneration and with limits to livestock production. At the same time, a program for the conservation of ecosystems and protection of the oceans is essential to stop the extinction of species and, through suitable crops and reforestation, create efficient natural carbon sinks.

How much time is there?

Until 2020. After that threshold, the inertia of CO_2, plus methane and nitrous oxide accumulated, will be combined with the defrosting of permafrost and the release of underwater clathrates, accelerated all by the absence of the albedo effect after thawing of the North Pole in the summers. If extreme measures are not taken immediately, the result will be the flooding of all coastal cities and the end of known civilization.

These measures are immediately applicable, within a situation similar to a world war economy. The objective is to drastically reduce carbon pollution, which is currently around 50 billion tons per year of emissions to the atmosphere and thus stop the activation of the "methane pump", at the same time invest heavily in alternative energy replacement and reforestation These two strategies will allow us to return to normal within 10 years if they are carried out intensively. **Political leaders must prepare and mentalize in order to face the macro scale of this global challenge.**

PLAN B - EVACUATION OF COASTAL CITIES

There is scientific consensus that the floating ice of the North Pole will be completely thawed in the summer of approximately 2030. Then, the albedo effect will no longer be present, the sun's rays will not bounce back into the high atmosphere, the waters of the Arctic

Ocean will start to overheat and a chain reaction will begin causing the release of the immense deposits of underwater methane gas hydrates and the continental permafrost. With which the average temperature of the planet will rise 6º C and up to 12º C in both poles, accelerating this the melting of the glacier massifs. Defrosting the ice in Greenland will make the oceans rise up to 7 meters and those in Antarctica up to 60 meters. This will happen abruptly in a period not exceeding 5 years.

So, do we have time until 2030 to apply preventive and corrective measures to the situation chart?

Do not! The answer depends on the critical threshold for the abrupt release of methane gas at the North Pole. The chain reaction is likely to start when the floating ice is reduced to 50% or a little more. And at the beginning, methane, 23 times more efficient than CO_2 in heating the atmosphere will further accelerate the defrosting of the ice in the North Pole. This temporarily places us between the years 2025 to 2027.

What possibilities do we have to stop this chain reaction?

We have time until 2020. We must declare a state of global emergency, reduce carbon emissions globally by 80%. Directly ban vehicles to explosion and move to electric and hydrogen. Plant 30 billion kiri trees per year and build thousands of giant CO_2 exhaust fans.

If we do not do this immediately, we must go to **Plan B: evacuate the coastal cities, when the waters begin to rise.** Convene governments and the Armed Forces and plan the logistics for the transfer of hundreds of millions of people to the highlands, foreseeing their vital support and the post-flood organization of each coastal country. Move the industrial parks located in connection with the ports and provide alternative maritime stations to continue international maritime traffic.
If we continue as before, in complete inaction and increasing carbon pollution, we will accelerate the process even more.

If measures beyond 2020 are applied, the inertia of CO_2 already released into the atmosphere plus the inertia of our civilization's consumption system will not allow us to stop the chain reaction of methane release at the North Pole.

Likewise, it is extremely important that the 2% Plan for the Planet be applied, trying to stabilize the temperature at an average of 4° C and not 6° or 8° C, which would be catastrophic.

It is up to the IPCC scientific panel to determine how much time we have left before the abrupt release of methane accumulated in the North Pole and then decide to declare the planetary emergency.

We are in this situation because we underestimate the problem. We thought we had more time. We must rethink that we have been discussing global warming for the last 40 years and if we know anything, Nature does not forgive!

ONE CATASTROPHE PER WEEK

According to the United Nations, climate catastrophes are occurring at a rate of one each week. The cost of climate-related disasters amounts to US $ 520 billion per year, while the additional cost of building infrastructure resistant to the effects of global warming is approximately 3%, that is, US $ 2 , 7 billion in total over the next 20 years.

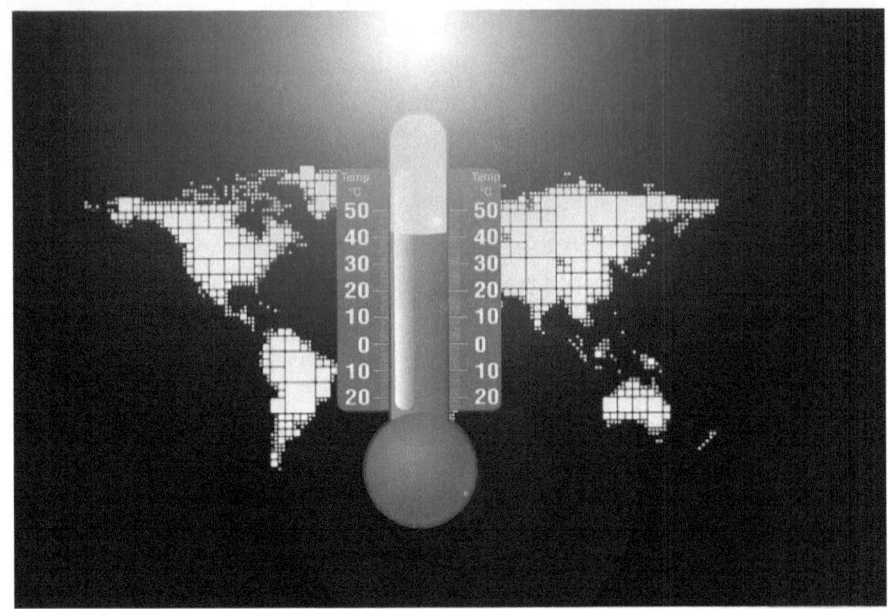

THE ARTIC METHANE PUMP: NOTE TO IPCC

Vast methane deposits, a greenhouse gas 23 times more potent than carbon dioxide, are found under permafrost and as global temperatures rise and permafrost falls apart, it could spread and accelerate the pace of climate change.

The uncertainty reveals the biggest problem in trying to understand what impact climate change will have on the Arctic permafrost and what effect the permafrost thaw will have on climate change and on underwater clathrates, scientists still do not have enough data to make predictions valid. For this reason we send the following note to the Intergovernmental Panel on Climate Change (IPCC).

NOTE TO IPCC

E-mail sent: ipcc-media@wmo.int

Dear IPCC Scientific Committee:

According to the study, published in the journal Environmental Research Letters, 17,000 years ago, at the end of the Pleistocene era, carbon gases, which occur naturally, escaped the seabed and altered both the Earth's atmosphere that melted the ice age.

"Currently, underwater carbon reservoirs release greenhouse gases into the atmosphere as the oceans heat up due to human activity. If underwater carbon deposits are altered again, they will emit a huge new source of greenhouse gases, which would exacerbate climate change," said Lowell Stott, professor of Earth sciences at the University of Southern California (USA) and lead author of the study, cited by the phys.org portal.

"The big challenge is that we have no estimates of the size of these or which are particularly vulnerable to destabilization. It is something that remains to be determined. The last time it happened, the climate change was so great that it caused the end of the ice age. Once that geological process begins, we will not be able to stop it" Stott warned.

"At the current rate of carbon dioxide increase in the atmosphere, the planet is likely to experience several degrees of global temperature increase and large-scale changes such as the loss of ice sheets that could lead to an increase in the level of sea of several meters in this century ", according to Dr. James Hansen.

"Two degrees Celsius of warming would make a planet Earth much warmer than during the Eemiano, and it would take it closer to the Pliocene conditions, when the sea level was about 25 meters higher than today," said Hansen.

In a few more years the North Pole will thaw completely during the summers. The albedo effect will no longer be present and the waters of the Arctic Ocean will start to overheat, so the huge deposits of methane and permafrost gas hydrates, 23 times more efficient than greenhouse CO_2, will begin to be released from the sea floor into the atmosphere. . The global average temperature may rise to 6° C and 12° C at both poles, whereby the glaciers will defrost at an accelerated rate.

The Secretary General of the United Nations, António Guterres, is calling all the governments of the planet to urgent Climate Action. In this regard, the support of a core scientific report on the Arctic permafrost cycle, carbohydrates in the Arctic and carbon reservoirs in the oceans is required.

 In order for the world to mobilize, science must answer the following questions:

1- How much carbon and methane are stored in the underwater bed and in the Arctic Circle?

2- If all of this methane and carbon is released into the atmosphere, how many degrees will the global average temperature increase especially over the poles?

3- With this higher temperature, what will be the defrosting rate of the glacier massifs in Greenland and Antarctica?

4- Is there already a process for the release of gases from permafrost and methane gas hydrates in the Arctic?

5- How much more should the temperature rise and the albedo effect be reduced so that the chain reaction of the release of Arctic underwater methane gas hydrates is initiated?

6- How many years are left before this chain reaction begins?

7- Can you guarantee that it will not happen?

8- Do you have empirical, statistical, probabilistic, comparative data to evaluate the phenomenon?

9- What do you recommend doing if the data is insufficient?

10- Do you support the 2% initiative for the Planet? (more info at https://2porcientoporelplaneta.home.blog/2019/07/15/e-gobierno-mundial/)

Currently, the United Nations is talking about organizing the efforts of all countries to reduce carbon emissions by 45% before 2030 and reach zero emissions by 2050. This objective may be insufficient, if we are at a short distance from the Critical threshold for abrupt chain reaction, release of methane gas in the Arctic Circle and carbon in the other oceans of the world. If this is the case, it will be necessary to reach zero emissions immediately.

We notify: Extinction Rebellion Argentina, Ecohouse, Aclimatando, Agenda Ambiental, Amartya, Animal Libre, Climate Save Argentina, Isla Verde, Juventud Ecologista, Fundación Solis, Greta Thunberg, Senadora Ocasio Cortez, WWF, Greenpeace, C40, CDP, Climate Network, Avina, The Climate Group, Wemean Business Coalition, Bteam

---

Fridays For Future Participation

FFF is a global movement that recognizes the climatic emergency and wants a safe road below 1.5° C.

Hi! Thanks for contacting #Fridaysforfuture.
You are asking some very interesting questions.
However, Fridaysforfuture is not an organization. It is a movement of people, and no person or body of people has the authority to sign this for FFF. Some countries may, and individuals active in FFF may want. If you inform us how to sign, we can transmit it through social networks.
Hoping this is of some help.

Sincerely,
Monica

Fridays For Future International<fridaysforfuture.int@gmail.com>

Contact with the Chilean Ministry of Environment

We communicate with the Ministry of Environment of Chile, the body responsible for the organization of COP25, we ask you to give this note to the delegations of the concurrent countries to sign it and send it to the IPCC

Reply:

Hereby, and under the framework established in Law No. 19.880, we respond to your inquiry registered in our application management system with No. 4-2019-OC-47, informing you of the following:

First of all, thank you very much for contacting us. The celebration of COP25 will be a tremendous challenge, in which we need the help of all citizens. This event will be a meeting point for the different sectors, to discuss and implement the necessary actions in the face of climate change. Without a doubt, it will be a great moment for Chile and the whole world.

By celebrating and organizing this event in our country, we will lead one of the most important transformations that our planet requires, in the path of sustainability and climate action.

Regarding your suggestion, we comment that all proposals are welcome, so contact has been made with the COP25 technical team to manage the delivery of the material that accompanies us in your requirement, to whom you point.

Contact with the United Nations Environment Program

Inger Andersen, Executive Director of the United Nations Environment Program and Deputy Secretary General of the United Nations.

Hi Inger Andersen! I appeal to your kindness and common sense to request you to send this note to the IPCC. It is necessary that these scientific questions about the "Arctic methane pump" be answered before the COP25 meeting, so that the necessary measures can be taken.

CONSULTATION WITHOUT RESPONSE TO SCIENTISTS ABOUT AN ABRUPTED REMOVAL OF CLATRATES RELEASE IN 2025/30

We consulted about 30 leading scientists specializing in climatology and global warming from the United States, Canada, European Union and Australia, asking them to answer the same questions that we sent to the IPCC. We do not receive any response. Except for Professor **Peter Wadhams**, which we transcribe below: **"I suggest that you read my book:" A Farewell to Ice "(UK: Penguin, US: Oxford University Press). Chapter 9 is all about the Arctic underwater methane threat."**

Answer us within 2 to 3 years later, it may be too late ...

THE RISK OF WRONG TO FOLLOW GRETA THUNBERG

The international Fridays For Future movement, led by the Swedish Greta Thunberg, has set targets to reduce carbon pollution by 80% by 2030, set rates on carbon emissions, limit trade agreements to those countries that assume their commitments to limit warming below 1.5º C and produce information on ecology at the educational level. All this with the support of the IPCC scientists.

But is this the right way to avoid climate catastrophe? To begin with in terms of science, the question depends on which scientists to choose to listen to, since there are moderate and other alarming predictions about future environmental events on the planet. And they are related to the consideration of the immense deposits of carbon, methane gas and nitrous oxide in permafrost and clathrates in the Arctic. The unquestionable scientific data is that right now a large amount of permafrost is being thawed and methane gas is released into the atmosphere, at a rate of acceleration as the planet continues to heat up. If there is a chain effect of the release of these deposits, the global average temperature can rise sharply 6º C and up to 12º C at both poles, hence the accelerated global thaw. With the effect of all coastal cities flooded simultaneously. How far are we from this phenomenon ?: **Close!**

Then, reducing pollution 80% just by 2030, does not guarantee that the "methane bomb" effect will not be activated in the Arctic during that critical period, which will coincide with the disappearance of all floating ice on the North Pole during summers and the absence of the albedo effect, causing the overheating of the Arctic Ocean, collaborating for the release of underwater methane gas hydrates. What is prudent to do ?: **Act immediately.**

How? Adopting urgent and drastic measures, reducing pollution as much as possible, tending to zero emissions in the short term and reducing energy consumption to 50% at the same time. Ban cars that consume fossil fuels and replace them in cities with electric urban transport vehicles. In other words, no more individual vehicles, it is a luxury of overconsumption that Nature no longer allows us. Minimize flights by plane. Ban tourism, one of the most polluting industries. Reduce the intake of red meat per inhabitant.

Replace the manufacturing concept "used and thrown away" with long-lasting objects of use. Turn off the lights of all cities after 8 pm. Replace thermal power plants that work by burning oil and coal, wind and solar. Move from intensive to organic crops. Accelerate fusion reactors. Invest heavily in alternative energies. Reforest by planting 30 billion trees per year, until reaching 500 billion and continue, because the technique is to cut the trunk once the tree grows to bury it and return CO2 to the subsoil and return to 350 ppm of this effect gas Free greenhouse in the atmosphere, returning to global climate normality.

And let's review the priorities: the goal is not to reduce emissions by 80% by 2030, but to save the Arctic. Prevent by all means at our disposal that the floating ice of the North Pole is completely defrosted during the summers. Because if that happens, the albedo effect will disappear, the ocean will overheat in surface up to 7° C and the bottom clathrates containing methane gas will begin to be released, starting an unstoppable positive feedback that will increase the global average temperature to 6° C, defrosting to Greenland... The second priority is to save Amazonia, which provides 20% of the world's oxygen and that if all its trees were burned, the temperature would rise by 1° C average... and the third is to find an abundant, cheap and accessible alternative energy source. This is found in fusion reactors. To obtain it, intensive investment is needed, such as the one applied in the Manhattan Project and the Apollo Program. But this time not less than 1 trillion dollars. We already need this capacity and we cannot postpone it.

THE ECONOMIC SYSTEM IN TOTAL COLLAPSE

According to Dr. James Hansen when 450 ppm of CO_2 is reached, in 2030, the global average temperature will rise 2° C, then the oceans can rise 6 meters or more. This new world situation will cause a disruption over the entire global economic and fiscal system. In addition to causing the evacuation of 600 million people in the coastal cities of the planet.

The physical assets, the real estate of all those sites will be worth zero overnight, much earlier, when the information that the phenomenon of global flooding begins to spread through scientific spokespersons, the properties on the coast will begin to lose value in cascade and the holders of these will stop paying their taxes to the municipal, provincial and national states. A crack will occur on the collection system.

Months and years before the waters cover the cities, people will be held captive in the damned cities, without the possibility of emigrating to the highlands, because they will not be able to sell their houses, since they will have lost all market value.

Defrosting will be slow and gradual, it will take several years. First the waterfront will run. The beach will disappear, then the pavement of the waterfront will be covered, later the sewage and storm systems, along with the basements of the buildings located in the lowest sites will begin to flood and its foundations will lose stability and fall apart. Then the sea water will begin to flow along the gutter until it climbs the path and wins the entrances of the houses.

It will be enough for an agency like the IPCC to officially report that this level of flooding cannot be stopped and that it will begin in the medium term, so that the value of the properties collapses and the economic system goes into a panic and total collapse. What to do? Do not inform and keep silent? Then urgent measures will not be taken and cities will be condemned to flood ... **what is worse?**

7th MASS EXTINCTION WITH 1 MILLION SPECIES IN DANGER

According to scientists we have entered the 7th mass extinction of species on Earth, caused by human predatory activity. During the last 500 years 680 vertebrate species disappeared, but in the next decades it is estimated that around one million animal and plant species will disappear. The report was prepared by international scientists for the United Nations Organization.

Species extinction levels in the next decades will be hundreds of times higher and fulminant than the average of the last 10 million years. Among the most vulnerable living beings are insects, responsible for the pollination of plants. Large chains of ecosystems will be threatened by this mass extinction, unless action is taken. The effects will begin to manifest with intensity from 2030.

DR. JAMES HANSEN: OCEANS CAN ASCEND 6 MINIMUM MINIMUM WITH 450 PPM CO2

"If humanity wishes to conserve a planet similar to that in which our civilization developed and for which life on Earth is adapted, paleoclimatic evidence and ongoing climate change suggest that (current levels of) CO_2 will have to be reduced to a maximum of 350 ppm", said **Dr. James Hansen**, an American physicist and climatologist, associate professor in the Department of Terrestrial and Environmental Sciences at Columbia University.

Hansen reflects that while fossil energy is the cheapest, the problem of climate change cannot be solved. That is why the capital system develops hydraulic fracturing (fracking) to obtain more gas and more oil. The situation will not change until carbon taxes are imposed.

He warns that when 450 ppm of CO_2 is reached, the sea level will rise a minimum of 6 meters, but it is unknown how quickly the ice will respond, since the composition of the atmosphere never varied as quickly as now.

50 million years ago the CO₂ level doubled and the planet warmed up 6° C more, but it took 2,000 years to do so. But with human pollution, CO₂ has now doubled in just a century.

If it reaches 450 ppm of CO₂ there will be two degrees Celsius of warming and this would make a planet Earth much warmer than during the Eemiano, and it would take it closer to the Pliocene conditions, when the sea level was about 25 meters higher than today, said Hansen. Using Earth's climate history, we learn more about the level of sensitivity that governs the planet's response to today's warming. Hansen said that the paleoclimatic record suggests that each Celsius degree that rises in global temperature could eventually mean 20 meters of sea level rise. However, that the sea level increases due to the loss of the ice sheet would be expected to occur for centuries, and great uncertainties remain in the prediction of how the loss of ice will originate.

UNCOVERED GREENHOUSE EFFECT

Dr. James Hansen warns that global warming could accelerate and enter a phase called "runaway", leading to a global climate situation similar to the planet Venus, where all the water contained in the oceans would evaporate and become integrated into the atmosphere producing a more potent greenhouse effect than CO₂, raising the surface temperature of the Earth to an average of 100° C, with which the planet would become completely hostile for all life. It would be the end and a path without return. Irreversible. For this, first all ice from the glaciers of both poles must be defrosted and at the same time the huge deposits of permafrost methane gas and underwater methane gas hydrates, as it is already happening, but in a more abrupt and accelerated way.

On the other hand, while Greenland and Antarctica are releasing more fresh and cold water, the North Atlantic and the Antarctic Ocean cool, increasing the temperature difference between low and high latitudes, which increases the strength of the storms. To this is added the increase in sea level and the consequent flooding of coastal cities, with the effect of a global economic collapse.

CARBON UNDERWATER RESERVES CAN BE RELEASED

They have discovered immense deposits of carbon gases trapped in the seabed. Some of them escaped, according to a scientific study published in the Environmental Reseach Letters magazine, at the end of the Pleistocene era, 17,000 years ago and this caused the end of the Ice Age. Changes in the atmosphere, in the temperature and pressure of the oceans can alter the underwater carbon cycle and cause a new massive release of these gases exacerbating global warming.

There is currently an active process of releasing these gases as the oceans continue to heat up due to human pollution. The main deposit is in the Eastern Equatorial Pacific, but more and more carbon deposits are being discovered in the deep oceans, near hydrothermal sources, without having precise information about its magnitude or vulnerability to destabilization. Once the release process starts, nothing can stop it.

Lowell D. Stott, a professor at the University of Southern California says that **"there are deposits of liquid and solid carbon dioxide that accumulate at the bottom of the ocean, within rocks and sediments at the margins of active waters. These sites, the volcanic magma that is found inside the Earth is found with superheated water, producing plumes of fluids rich in carbon dioxide that seep through the cracks in the earth's crust and migrate to the surface."**

He also indicated that **"when a pen of this fluid encounters cold sea water, carbon dioxide can solidify in a form called hydrate. The hydrate forms a cap that traps carbon dioxide inside rocks and sediments and prevents it from entering the ocean. But at temperatures above approximately 48 degrees Fahrenheit (9 degrees Celsius), the hydrate will melt, releasing floating liquid or gaseous carbon dioxide directly into the overlying water."**

He said that **"carbon dioxide levels in the atmosphere increased rapidly at the end of each of the late Pleistocene ice ages, helping to warm the weather. During the most recent warming episode 17,000 years ago, Earth warmed from 9 to 13 degrees Fahrenheit (5 to 7 degrees Celsius). The Paleocene-Eocene thermal maximum warmed the planet so dramatically that the rainforests extended north to the Arctic."**

THE TOTAL DEVELOPMENT OF THE ARTICO IS INEVITABLE

Peter Wadhams, Professor of Ocean Physics and Head of the Polar Ocean Physics Group of the Department of Applied Mathematics and Theoretical Physics at the University of Cambridge, argues that the total melting of the Arctic in summer is virtually inevitable in summer (more than 20 degrees have already been recorded Celsius above average for a few weeks). This will cause an exponential acceleration of global warming due to the absence of the albedo effect, the overheating of the Arctic Ocean waters, the possible release of methane gas hydrates and the accelerated defrosting of Greenland's glaciers. All this would happen from 2025/30, according to the global scientific consensus.

If methane is released in the Arctic according to the amounts proposed by Shakhova and Semiletov, Wadhams estimates that climate warming can increase 0.6° C in a decade. He said that methane is already being released at accelerated levels in the Eastern Siberian Sea as in the Láptev Sea and the Barent Sea. Scientifically it is proven that the amount of methane emerging from the seabed is rising. The question is how much it can continue to increase. Recent observations from the United States and Russia details vast columns of methane bubbles that are already released from beneath the East Siberian platform in waters 60 m deep. Once the summer sea ice disappears completely, the consequent warming of the Arctic can cause the release of a pulse of approximately 50 gigatons of methane over a period of a few years, according to studies cited by Wadhams. And about the reason why the IPCC does not consider the issue, he thinks it is because **"they do not want to cause panic."**

The scientist explains that even if carbon emissions are stopped, as it is a slow inertia greenhouse gas, with the amount already poured into the atmosphere, it will also reach 2º C. Therefore, the question is how to start extracting it, not just stop issuing. If the emissions do not stop, according to the IPCC it will reach 4º C at the end of this century and the capacity of food production for the total population will be lost. He also indicated that pollution is an effect of capitalism, but there is no time to change the system, since warming is now and we must solve the problem in the present tense.

PLANT 30 THOUSAND MILLION TREES PER YEAR TO REMOVE CO2 AND RETURN TO 350 PPM FREE IN THE ATMOSPHERE

From 30 to 50 billion tons / year of carbon dioxide are emitted into the atmosphere. By planting 30 billion kiri trees per year, 30 billion tons of CO_2 / year can be captured.
The forests will reverse.

You can plant 30 billion new kiri trees per year and then bury the logs, trap the CO_2 and return this greenhouse gas to the subsoil and proceed to an intelligent control of the global climate, regulating the free carbon dioxide in the atmosphere. Making green forests of the planet green. The task will be carried out by the multinational AEON of Japan, with experience in forest recovery, so as not to repeat the mistakes made with the green credits. Global warming is turning the frozen deserts of Canada and Siberia nortes, into areas suitable for new forests, so agricultural areas will not be invaded in the development of this project.

U$S 30 billion will be allocated per year for this purpose. The Global Reforestation project will allow to move from the climate crisis to the complete control of the planetary climate through the regulation of free CO_2 in the atmosphere. New techniques for massive plantations have been developed, using airplanes that machine the appropriate soils with seeds. Therefore, the recovery of forests can be carried out in the medium term and in the time of a generation to achieve that Humanity interact intelligently with the global climate, producing an adequate average temperature for the best sustainability.

The kiri tree can purify the infertile soil, it also absorbs 10 times more CO_2 than any other species.

It can reach up to 27 m high. It has 40 cm wide sheets. It resists fire by regenerating its rapidly growing roots and vessels and also tolerates pollution. It is not necessary to replant as it sprouts after cutting. It thrives in contaminated soils and waters and purifies the soil as it grows, from its leaves, rich in nitrogen, provides nutrients by falling and decomposing in the soil.

An adult tree can capture 21.7 kg of CO_2 every day, which converts into 6 kg of oxygen.

30 billion adult kiri trees capture 651 billion kg of CO_2 per day, or 651,000 tons. A year there are 30 billion tons of CO_2 captured. As long as the intensive reforestation plan continues on the planet, the percentage of atmospheric CO_2 can be reduced between 1.5 and 2 ppm per year. In a maximum of 40 years, it would return to the ideal threshold of 350 ppm and return to the initial thermal equilibrium of the planet.

Kiri emits large amounts of oxygen and absorbs up to ten times more carbon dioxide than other trees.

The Intensive Global Reforestation Project initiative is undertaken by the United Nations, which manages international funds in coordination with nations with areas to be reforested.

Intensive global reforestation is concentrated in the areas of the Siberian tundra and Canada to the north, which due to global warming have become suitable for forest development. However, smaller projects focus on all nations to recover their native forests.

IMPACT OF THE PROJECT

30 billion adult kiri trees capture 651 billion kg of CO_2 per day, or 651,000 tons. A year there are 30 billion tons of CO_2 captured. As long as the intensive reforestation plan continues on the planet, the percentage of atmospheric CO_2 can be reduced between 1.5 and 2 ppm per year. In a maximum of 40 years, it would return to the ideal threshold of 350 ppm and return to the initial thermal equilibrium of the planet.

PROJECT COST

Project costs are equivalent to 30 billion dollars per year. To obtain these funds, a 0.1% financial rate will be established in the international and national financial system. These funds will be administered by the United Nations and by a commission composed of all nations added to the project.

TIMELINE

In the period of 1 to 15 years (short term): Reduce CO_2 pollution by 40% and stabilize the global average temperature below the threshold of 1.5° C.

In the period of 15 to 50 years (medium term): Reduce CO_2 pollution by 80% and stabilize the global average temperature below the 1.5° C threshold.

In the period of 50-100 years (long term): Return to 350 ppm of free CO_2 in the atmosphere and the global temperature will have fallen 1° C.

This strategy to capture CO_2 works, as long as the goal of zero emissions is implemented immediately.

DELTA SYSTEM

Environmental pollution is aggravated worldwide by a fleet of more than one billion vehicles with explosion engines, consuming hydrocarbons and eliminating the CO_2 atmosphere. This situation is repeated as a tracing in all cities. The solution directly involves replacing this form of transport with a more rational and less polluting one. Freeing even large cities from smog.

The Delta System allows the advantages of subways to be transferred by air. It consists of a series of arched arches of reinforced concrete, with a foundation base of the same material, fully prefabricated, installed at a distance of 25 meters each and joined by a hollow beam at the top. Through this route run the wagons, which can be by mechanical, electrical or levitated system.

The stops are every five blocks, at an elevated level and the system has a route every ten blocks inside the entire urban ejido. And it is designed to withstand curves at 25 meters, so that you can bend in apples.

Within this logic, all the inhabitants only have to walk a maximum of 10 blocks and it is admitted that the disabled and the elderly can travel in electric vehicles at street level. The entire individual car park is prohibited and the pavement streets are parked. Sound pollution and greenhouse gas emissions are eliminated. Also, the system has the advantage of rapid installation, since its infrastructure is completely prefabricated. The cars are intelligent, fully automated and run without a driver.

The cost of arcaded arches and the hollow beam per block is around 25% more than paving 100 meters one block.

Decommissioning the mass automotive industry is a pending decision that must be taken to curb Global Warming.

Either it is done, or all coastal cities are flooded and crops are lost, due to the increase in the global average temperature, at some point in the medium-term future.

PLANT MORE THAN 500,000 MILLION TREES

According to a study by a team led by researchers from the Institute of Integrative Biology of the Swiss Federal Institute of Technology in Zurich (ETH-Zurich), there is enough space to increase the forest area by 25% and thereby reduce the effect gases by 25% greenhouse in the atmosphere.

The goal is to plant at least 500 billion new trees. It is the cheapest and most effective method to capture CO2. There are currently about 3 billion live trees on the planet and we cut down around 15 billion per year, the surface of Portugal, not counting those that are lost due to burning by forest fires.

The maps and models generated by this team formed by experts from Switzerland, Italy and France indicate that there is sufficient area to increase the forest mass by 25% without this representing irreversible damage to agricultural production or natural ecosystems.

The researchers used Google Earth to see in which areas more trees could be planted, while maintaining space for people (agriculture and urbanized areas) and natural ecosystems. Jean-Francois Bastin explains that they have calculated that there is room for at least one billion more trees, but they could be 1.5 billion.

About two thirds of the entire Earth - 8.6 billion hectares - could sustain forests and 5.5 billion already sustain them. Of the 3.2 billion without trees, 1.5 billion are used for cultivation, leaving 1.6 billion hectares of potential forest land in areas that were previously degraded or sparsely vegetated, where 1,200,000,000 native trees could grow. That area is about 11% of the entire Earth and equals the size of the United States and China together. Tropical areas could have 100% tree cover, while others would be more sparsely covered, which means that, on average, approximately half of the area would be under forest cover.

The objective of an increase of 25% forestry will allow the capture of 200 gigatons of carbon. It is the cheapest solution to curb climate change. This strategy must be accompanied by cuts in carbon emissions so that positive results are obtained against global warming.

The six largest nations in the world, Russia, Canada, China, the United States, Brazil and Australia, contain half of the possible restoration sites. Tree planting initiatives already exist, including the Bonn Challenge, backed by 48 nations, aimed at restoring 350 million hectares of forest by 2030. The United Nations launched the "Trillion Tree Campaign" campaign, so far more than 17,000 million trees in the world.

ETHIOPIA BREAKS WORLD RECORD WHEN PLANTING MORE THAN 350 MILLION TREES IN ONE DAY

In less than a day, Ethiopia broke a world record by planting 350 million trees in just 12 hours. The incident occurred on July 29, 2019. 3 million people participated. The seedlings were planted as part of a campaign convened by the Gulele Botanical Garden of Addis Ababa to combat the effects of deforestation and climate change.

The initiative corresponded to the Green Legacy of Ethiopian Prime Minister Abiy Ahmed. The first idea and objective was to plant 200 million trees in 1,000 different places in the country, in a single day. But the enthusiasm of the collaborators exceeded the initial expectations. Achieving breaking the previous record held by India since 2016, with 50 million trees.

Ethiopia during the previous century had 35% forested. Due to logging, this percentage was reduced to 4%.

According to research published in the journal Science, if one billion hectares of forest are reforested, two thirds of all emissions that have been released into the atmosphere since the 19th century could be eliminated as a result of human activities (approximately 300 gigatons)).

The feat of Ethiopia encourages hope. If 350 million trees can be planted in 12 hours in a single country, repeating this in almost 200 countries, 60 billion new trees are reached to combat global warming. And if the effort lasts for 10 days it reaches 600 billion. This means that it is possible. It is within our means to achieve it. You just have to decide to do it.

Despite this, German Chancellor Angela Merkel has delayed until 2038 the closure of the last coal mine in the country.

GREENLAND DEFROST IT UP AND BELOW

Scientists estimate that the total disappearance of the Arctic ice sheet would mean an elevation of 7 meters from the global sea level. As the air temperature rises above Greenland, the thaw accelerates exponentially for each degree of increase in the atmosphere. The loss of the glacier massifs of both poles and their surface layer adds 660 gigatons of water per year to the ocean, equivalent to 268 million Olympic swimming pools. Not only does sea level rise, ocean currents are altered.

IN 2019 GERMANY REDUCED 15% ITS EMISSIONS

For the first time in Germany renewable energy sources produced more electricity than coal and nuclear energy combined. In the first six months of 2019, solar, wind, biomass and hydroelectric power generation accounted for 47.3 percent of the country's electricity production, while 43.4 percent came from coal and nuclear power plants. .

According to figures published by the Fraunhofer Institute for Solar Energy Systems (ISE) in July, about 15% less carbon dioxide was produced than in the same period last year. The production of electricity from solar panels increased by six percent, natural gas by 10 percent. The use of black coal decreased by 30 percent compared to the first half of 2018, and lignite, a substance similar to coal formed from peat, decreased by 20 percent.

Its renewable energy has steadily increased over the past two decades thanks in part to the Renewable Energy Law (EEG), which was amended last year to reduce costs for consumers.

This German achievement of reducing emissions by 15% is the goal for all countries. In this way in just 6 years a global reduction of 90% would be achieved.

TOURISM, GREAT POLLUTOR

The tourism industry accounts for approximately 8% of global carbon emissions and absorbs 10.5% of the planet's GDP. Between 2009 and 2013, the carbon footprint of international tourism increased 3.9 to 4.5 Gt CO2 - equivalent, four times more than previously estimated.

The number of cruise passengers went from 17.8 million in 2009 to 27.2 in 2018. The increase in just 9 years was 52.8%.
It is estimated that a cruise ship with a capacity of 2,000-3,000 passengers can generate about 1,000 tons of waste every day, which are divided as follows:
- 550,000-800,000 liters of gray water
- 100,000-115,000 liters of sewage
- 13,500-26,000 liters of oily bilge water
- 7,000-10,500 kilos of garbage and solid waste
- 60-130 kilos of toxic waste

The fuel consumption of a cruise ship is equivalent to that of 12,000 vehicles, with the aggravating fact that the type of fuel used in most of these ships is 50 times more toxic than usual. There are currently about 230 cruises.

For its part, the plane assuming, for example, that it has 88 people on board, it would be that it emits 285 grams of CO2 per passenger and kilometer. While the train is the one that wins, since it would emit only 14 grams of carbon dioxide and would be the one that would transport more people: 156.

Another negative effect of tourism is the excessive construction on the coastal strip exposed to erosion.

THE NEW HUMAN DIET

By 2030 the world will contain 8600 million inhabitants and human beings will necessarily have to modify their eating habits. Popular diets that have been consumed for the past 50 years are not nutritionally optimal, damage the environment and accelerate the erosion of natural biodiversity. A healthier diet would reduce premature deaths by 23%.

The main change is to reduce the intake of red meat, limiting it to 14/28 g per day. And increase the consumption of legumes, nuts, fruits and vegetables to 100%.

Almost one billion people are hungry, and almost 2 billion people eat too much food. Unhealthy diets are responsible for up to 11 million preventable premature deaths per year.

A LIGHT OF HOPE

In September 2019, Germany launched a € 54 billion plan to combat the climate crisis. The objective is to achieve a reduction of 55% of CO2 emissions by 2030 compared to 1990.

On the other hand, the giant Amazon, led by Jeff Bezos, who delivers more than 10,000 million items a year, has set out to comply with the Paris agreement ten years before and invites all other companies to imitate it. To achieve this, it has announced the purchase of 100,000 electric vehicles for deliveries, a fleet that will be in full circulation in 2030. By the same date it will use only renewable energy. It will also invest in forest reforestation, allocating $ 100 million through The Nature Conservancy to launch the Right Now Climate Fund, which will provide financial resources to recover and protect forests, wetlands and peatlands worldwide.

SUMMARY

WMO predicts that between 2020 and 2023 there is a 10% chance of a global temperature rise to 1.5° C. This means that the UN goal of not exceeding this threshold will not be heard by the warming pace itself Global acceleration. While by 2030 it will reach 450 ppm of CO2, if we continue at the same rate of pollution, and as a result the fateful 2° C that will activate the positive feedbacks that will cause the abrupt defrosting of the Arctic continental permafrost and then of the underwater clathrates, which they already accuse an active defrosting process. At the same time the floating ice of the North Pole will have disappeared during the summers, together with the albedo effect and the Arctic Ocean will be reheating to 5° / 7° C activating the release of methane gas hydrates from the bottom. Then the global temperature will skyrocket at ~ 4° / 6° C and up to 12° C at both poles, beginning the accelerated thaw of Greenland and Antarctica, being able to rise the oceans up to 60 meters in years and not in millennia, flooding all the coastal cities and causing 600 million simultaneous environmental refugees.

If we want to avoid this catastrophe we must carry out a double coordinated action. On the one hand reduce carbon emissions and on the other reduce energy consumption per capita and extract CO2. To curb the inertia of CO2 already underway we must make an extraordinary effort of zero emissions immediately. To achieve this, individual vehicles that run on fossil fuels in cities must be banned and replaced by urban passenger transport, possibly electric or hydrogen. Prohibit tourism. Turn off the lights of all cities at 20 hours. Reduce by 80% the consumption of red meat. Replace intensive crops with organic ones. Invest intensively in alternative energies. Plant no less than 30 billion kiri trees per year, and then cut down their logs and bury them by returning the sequestered CO2 to the subsoil.

Within the Climate Emergency it is necessary to include that the great ecological reserves of the planet, on which the global ecosystem depends, become of international jurisdiction under the administration of the United Nations. What happened with the fires in Amazonia, has served as an example about the irresponsibility of what "can" national sovereignty over the "green lung" of all Humanity.

It is imperative to abandon the idea that we can successfully face the challenge of Global Warming with all the comforts of today's consumer society. We must leave the comfort zone and many amenities to which we are accustomed. We have no other alternative. We must apply drastic cuts to our individual consumption habits to achieve effective global results. And the most difficult, perhaps, of all, install in the world society the practice of only one child per family. The planet can only support 5,000 billion. We must reduce the current overpopulation. Being more and more, the problems increase. If we do not accept the challenge and continue to pollute and overpopulate, we run the risk of unbalancing the global ecosystem of the planet to the point where it is not more suitable for sustaining life.

It is a fatal mistake to propose a 45% reduction in emissions by 2030 or 80%. If we want climate security we must apply zero emissions from 2020 and thus stop the eco-systemic feedback.

We will be 8,600 million inhabitants by 2030 and between 10,000 and 12,000 million by 2050. Energy consumption will then have increased 50% and 100% respectively. With these levels of demand it is unlikely to reach zero emissions by 2050, developing renewable energy up to 85% of the world's electricity. The idea of needing an area the size of Australia to devote to energy crops will be insufficient if demand continues to grow under the pressure of overpopulation. We would need to double that surface, which is irrational and impracticable. Then it is urgent and imperative to do two simultaneous things: 1. Reduce energy consumption to 50%. 2. Reduce overpopulation to 5,000 billion by limiting the number of children to only one per family. This must be understood, we must do it yes or yes, we have no other alternative. In case we do not do it, our planetary ecosystem will collapse completely and the 7th mass extinction will come that will include us all.

Let us repeat the concept of what needs to be done so that it is understood: We have turned a huge amount of CO_2 into the atmosphere, which is a slow inertia gas. That means that even if we stop contaminating, the temperature will continue to rise and the dreaded positive natural feedback from ecosystems will trigger, generating more warming and defrosting of permafrost, methane and ice. To stop this cycle, zero emissions must be applied immediately. To achieve this, you have to reduce energy consumption to 50%, apply a massive investment in replacement alternatives and plant 500 billion kiri trees to extract atmospheric CO_2. It is within our means to do so. We will not like it. But it is the effective remedy for Global Warming disease and to this we add that no family can have more than one child. Move to the overpopulation limitation and return to 5,000 billion inhabitants by 2075.

50% of corals have already died, we kill 50% of the fish, we kill 60% of the biodiversity, we cut half of all the forests, we pollute all the oceans, the temperature rose more than 1° C and several degrees more in both poles, which are already defrosting, like permafrost and clathrates, rainforests and forests are catching fire, there are intense and recurring hurricanes and droughts, rivers and lakes dry, glaciers thaw. All ecosystems are falling apart and we continue to react, **will we wait until the water reaches our knees and we don't have to eat?**

BIBLIOGRAPHIC REFERENCES

IPCC (2007). «2.3 Climate sensitivity and feedbacks». En Pachauri, R.K and Reisinger, A. (eds.). Climate Change 2007: Synthesis Report. Contribution of Working Groups I, II and III to the Fourth Assessment Report of the Intergovernmental Panel on Climate Change. Ginebra, Suiza: Intergovernmental Panel on Climate Change.

Prentice, I.C. et al (2001). «Technical Summary: F.3 Projections of Future Changes in Temperature». En Houghton J.T. et al (Eds.). Climate Change 2001: The Scientific Basis. Contribution of Working Group I to the Third Assessment Report of the Intergovernmental Panel on Climate Change. Ginebra, Suiza: Intergovernmental Panel on Climate Change..

Knutti, Reto; Hegerl, Gabriele C. (26 de octubre de 2008). «The equilibrium sensitivity of the Earth's temperature to radiation changes». Nature Geoscience 1 (11): 735-743. doi:10.1038/ngeo337.

Randall, D.A., et al (2007). «8.6.2 Interpreting the Range of Climate Sensitivity Estimates Among General Circulation Models, In: Climate Models and Their Evaluation». En Solomon, S., D. et al (Eds.). Climate Change 2007: Synthesis Report. Contribution of Working Groups I, II and III to the Fourth Assessment Report of the Intergovernmental Panel on Climate Change. Cambridge University Press, Cambridge.

Prentice, I.C. et al (2001). «9.2.1 Climate Forcing and Climate Response, in chapter 9. Projections of Future Climate Change». En Houghton J.T. et al (eds.). Climate Change 2001: The Scientific Basis. Contribution of Working Group I to the Third Assessment Report of the Intergovernmental Panel on Climate Change. Cambridge University Press, Cambridge, United Kingdom and New York, NY, USA. ISBN 9780521807678.

Solomon, S., D. et al (eds.) (2007). «Glossary A-D, Climate sensitivity». Contribution of Working Group I to the Fourth Assessment Report of the Intergovernmental Panel on Climate Change, 2007. Cambridge University Press, Cambridge, United Kingdom and New York, NY, USA.

Rahmstorf, Stefan (2008). «Anthropogenic Climate Change: Revisiting the Facts» (PDF). En Zedillo, E. Global Warming: Looking Beyond Kyoto. Brookings Institution Press. pp. 34-53.

Ad Hoc Study Group on Carbon Dioxide and Climate (1979). «Carbon Dioxide and Climate: A Scientific Assessment» (PDF). National Academy of Sciences.

V. Ramanathan, M.S. Lian, and R.D. Cess (1979). Increased Atmospheric CO2: Zonal and Seasonal Estimates of the Effect on Radiative Energy Balance and Surface Temperature (PDF). Journal of Geophysical Research.

O. Boucher, et al (2001). «6.3.1 Carbon Dioxide in: Chapter 6 Radiative Forcing of Climate Change». En Houghton J.T. et al (eds.). Climate Change 2001: The Scientific Basis. Contribution of Working Group I to the Third Assessment Report of the Intergovernmental Panel on Climate Change. Cambridge University Press, Cambridge.

Collins, W. D., et al. (2006). «Radiative forcing by well-mixed greenhouse gases: Estimates from climate models in the Intergovernmental Panel on Climate Change (IPCC) Fourth Assessment Report (AR4)». J. Geophys.

John Farley (2008). «The Scientific Case for Modern Anthropogenic Global Warming». Monthly Review.

Ganopolski, A., and T. Schneider von Deimling (2008). «Comment on "Aerosol radiative forcing and climate sensitivity deduced from the Last Glacial Maximum to Holocene transition" by Petr Chylek and Ulrike Lohmann». Geophys.

Richard A. Kerr (13 de agosto de 2004). «Three Degrees of Consensus». Science 305 (5686): 932-4. PMID 15310873. doi:10.1126/science.305.5686.932.

Idso, Sherwood (1998). «CO2-induced global warming: A skeptic's view of potential climate change». Climate Research 10: 69-82. doi:10.3354/cr010069.

Gerhard, L.C.; Harrison, W.E.; Hanson, W.E. (2001). «Geological perspectives of global climate change». AAPG Special Publication SG47: 317-336.

Andronova, N.; Schlesinger, M. E. (2001). «Objective Estimation of the Probability Distribution for Climate Sensitivity». J. Geophys.

Forest, C.E.; Stone, P.H.; Sokolov, A.P.; Allen, M.R.; Webster, M.D. (2002). «Quantifying uncertainties in climate system properties with the use of recent observations"

Gregory, J.M.; Stouffer, R.J.; Raper, S.C.B.; Stott, P.A.; Rayner, N.A. (2002). «An observationally based estimate of the climate sensitivity». Journal of Climate

Shaviv, N.J. (2005). «On climate response to changes in the cosmic ray flux and radiative budget». J. Geophys.

K. Scherer, H. Fichtner, T. Borrmann, J. Beer, L. Desorgher, E. Flükiger, H.-J. Fahr, S. E. S. Ferreira, U. W. Langner, M. S. Potgieter, B. Heber, J. Masarik, N. J. Shaviv and J. Veizer (2006). «Interstellar-Terrestrial relations: Variable cosmic environments, the dynamic heliosphere, and their imprints on terrestrial archives and climate». Space Science

Frame, D.J.; Booth, B.B.B.; Kettleborough, J.A.; Stainforth, D.A.; Gregory, J.M.; Collins, M.; Allen, M.R. (2005). «Constraining climate forecasts: the role of prior assumptions». Geophysical Research Letters

Annan, J.D.; Hargreaves, J. C. (2006). «Using multiple observationally-based constraints to estimate climate sensitivity». Geophysical Research Letters

Forster, Piers M. de F.; Gregory, Jonathan M. (2006). «The Climate Sensitivity and Its Components Diagnosed from Earth Radiation Budget Data». Journal of Climate

Royer, Dana L.; Berner, Robert A.; Park, Jeffrey (29 de marzo de 2007). «Climate sensitivity constrained by CO2 concentrations over the past 420 million years». Nature

Sceptics as Jan Veizer have pointed out that while data for the whole Phanerozoic are available Royer et al. left out the time span younger than 420 Ma with an ice age and extremely high carbon dioxide content during the Hirnantian.

Prentice, I.C. et al (2001). «9.2.1 Climate Forcing and Climate Response, in chapter 9. Projections of Future Climate Change». En Houghton J.T. et al Eds. Climate Change 2001: The Scientific Basis. Contribution of Working Group I to the Third Assessment Report of the Intergovernmental Panel on Climate Change. Print version: Cambridge University Press. This version: GRID-Arendal website. ISBN 9780521807678.

«Target CO2». RealClimate. abril de 2008.

Roberto Gomes

Yogui Mettàtron

Architect / Journalist / Writer / Ecologist / Master in Yoga, Acupuncture, Osteopathy, Therapeutic Yoga and Mindfulness

Creator of NeuroYoga. Developer of the FlashBrain Program for the intellectual increase and the Synaptic Meditation technique. Promoter and leader of the initiative for 2% of world GDP, annually, to give a definitive solution to the triple scourge of hunger, overpopulation and global warming.

He was born in Argentina in 1956. He had his first spiritual trance at 16 years of age. At 17, the Virgin appeared to him and asked - Why do not you believe in Me? - Shortly after, the Cosmic Mother, he was awakening different states of high samadhis and had spiritual experiences very similar to those of Paramahansa Ramakrishna. At 19, he became a disciple of Yogananda and in meditation, he rediscovered the ancient technique of Kriya. He studied MT with the Maharishi and Zazen with the Bustamante teacher.

Yogi affirms that **"my experiences with God are the derivative of a contact with the essence of my own spiritual Being, since the soul and God share the same substrate of existence. They are a transcendent step in the knowledge of oneself. The phenomenon is it finds within the mental field and is its reflection".**

Subsequently, he completed his training as a graphic designer, journalist, hammer and public broker, fisherman sailor, architect, web designer and programmer, writer, master in yoga and creator of NeuroYoga.

On 02/02/04, after a prolonged period of meditation with the Vipassana technique, he reached mental cessation.

He designed the Sophia Cerebral Synergy system, through which it is possible to redesign the brain by stimulating neuroplasticity and increasing the IQ. He synthesized the Synaptic Meditation technique, through which accumulated stress is discharged, diseases are prevented and memory, attention and intelligence are increased, allowing the Supercerebro to function.

Its objective is to westernize the ancient spiritual knowledge of the East without losing the essence of its core, expanding and renewing research. Simplify meditation, making it available to everyone and laying the groundwork for its curricular introduction into world education systems.

The other focus is to unite actions to curb Global Warming-Flooding, while there is still time to apply preventive and corrective measures to the situation presented by greenhouse gases. At the same time expand compassion to address the scourge of hunger, which punishes more than one billion and educate to stop overpopulation.

"My mission: to serve humanity"

Yogi Mettàtron is western and Christian. He successfully achieved two careers in his life: one as a journalist, becoming editor-in-chief of a newspaper and the other as a practicing yogi. His work always focused on serving others. For him to serve is "the highest expression of Love." Through the teachings of Vedanta, he gradually discovered what the true goal of life was. On 02/02/04, after a prolonged period of meditation with the Vipassana technique, he reached mental cessation, when consciousness merges with the Absolute. I wanted to help people both physically, mentally and spiritually. That is how he created the Neuroyoga system, a synthesis yoga that creates the basis of modern yoga practice in the West.

The greatest treasure is knowledge

Writing became the new mission of For what could bring people more lasting help. His goal is to spread spiritual knowledge as much as possible. For him, knowledge is the greatest of all gifts. The words we hear are soon forgotten; Only the written word endures.

Holistic Neuroyoga

Teach the Neuroyoga from a holistic point of view: the Neuroyoga teaches us to strengthen and harmonize the body, mind and soul, so that we can reach the goal: a healthy body, a balanced mind and inner peace. The Neuroyoga helps eliminate inner obstacles and gives us strength to remain equanimous, calm and connected when we face the daily challenges of modern life.

Yogi.mettatron@gmail.com

www.ingramcontent.com/pod-product-compliance
Lightning Source LLC
Chambersburg PA
CBHW051414250726
48655CB00003B/1044